OUR DAILY DEBATES

NOTES TO THE TEXT

FOR FURTHER READING
AND DEBATES ABOUT
GRAPHIC DESIGN

COLOPHON

Working Title:

OUR DAILY DEBATES

Or:

45 MINUTES WITH GRAPHIC

DESIGNERS

REVISED 9/6 2007

1 INT. RIETVELD - GRAPHIC DESIGN STUDIO - ROOM 217 1

It is 7 weeks before graduation, A student (NINA 26) has asked 4 other students (SIRKEL 23, CLAUS 33, NOA 31, BRITA 30) to meet her and have a debate about graphic design, their future profession. NINA is pulling books and notes out of her bag, SIRKEL is working on his laptop. They are waiting for the others and looking at the time. There is coffee, tea and cookies on the table.
CLAUS enters.

CLAUS
Heeey, you've got cookies!

NINA
Yep, and coffee... You will need it!

As CLAUS is settling down NOA and BRITA enter. They are already having a loud discussion, NOA gesticulates wildly with a cigarette hanging on her lip.

NOA
Hey guys! So what's the question of today?...

Others laughing. General hustle and bustle as they settle down. They reach for coffee and small-talk a bit.

CUT TO

2 INT. RIETVELD - GRAPHIC DESIGN STUDIO - ROOM 217 2

They are in the middle of a discussion. Coffee-cups are scattered on the table.

CLAUS
It is very *fragile*, this discussion about graphic design...

SIRKEL

It's now what we are trying to *define* what we are studying here[1], defining what we learn in the three years and what we want to do *now*...

NINA

Yeah ... how we take that *outside* of the academy?

General murmur.

CLAUS

Yeah, it is a problem to find interesting work afterwards. I mean, how is that gonna... How is that going to work?

NINA

I think you just have to *make* it interesting.

SIRKEL

(laughing)

Did you hear what Linda[2] said to the Basic Year[3] students?

CLAUS

No?

SIRKEL

Well, they had this talk, where people from the Basic Year could ask questions about the graphic design department.

BRITA

Yeah.

SIRKEL

And Linda told them... She said...

BRITA
(joking)
You're not going to make any money...

SIRKEL (CONT'D)
(smiles)
One of the students from the Basic Year asked her; 'What's happening after you graduate from the design department at Rietveld?' Linda said; 'You have shitty work, shitty projects, shitty clients, shitty salary, shitty life, - but at least the school was good!'

Nervous laughter and comments, they look at each other, amused but also slightly tense.

CLAUS
(coughs)
No... We can't leave the academy with that remark...

SIRKEL
Yeah, I know ... good luck everybody...

NINA
Yeah...

NOA
Hey hey hey hey, what is that?!

SIRKEL
... I think it will be very difficult...

They lean back in silence and look at each other.

CUT TO

3 INT. RIETVELD - GRAPHIC DESIGN STUDIO - ROOM 217 3

They are sitting at the same table, but have changed seats. The coffee cups and the books on the table are the same, but in a different position.

SIRKEL
What we study here is so marginal.

BRITA
Noooo it is not!

NOA
(affirmingly)
It is marginal.

BRITA
In Sweden it is fucking marginal, here there is much more...

SIRKEL
Talk to any graphic designer who is not directly connected to the Rietveld Academy, and often they don't know who our teachers are...

BRITA
They have heard of Experimental Jetset[4]!?

NOA
No...

BRITA
But ... fuck ... it is not...
I know what you mean, but it is not comparable!

SIRKEL
It is not, it is not.

BRITA
Here in Holland people grew up with a certain *kind* of graphic design...

SIRKEL
Everybody knows graphic design here and even goes to graphic design exhibitions. But the design that we are studying *here*...

BRITA
(interrupts, loud)
It is *dying*, I tell you, it is dying out! But it is not marginal.

SIRKEL
It *is* marginal...

NINA
Define how it is marginal...

SIRKEL
What we study here at the Rietveld ... there is only a small group of people practising design like this - in the world, you know...

BRITA
But that does not mean that only *few* people know about it. I think a lot of people *wish* to do it, but you can easily fall for ... *money* ... or the 'we don't care'-thing. I think it is extremely few, like Linda or Julia[5] or René[6] or Jetsets, who *dares* to live a life where they really *live* for it, and that is what is inspiring us, but I don't think that everybody

graduating from here every year, is going to do that either. But we *know* about it, we are aware of it, and we are trying to do something about it... I cannot make any promises myself either... But I think I will ... you know, fight for it, I think...

CLAUS

But...

NINA

But what is so special about what we do? Can we define our education...?

BRITA

I think that a lot of it is that we *care* about the content, we *care* about the whole thing. We think that graphic design should start from the beginning of a project until the end... Also, what is the *quality* of the thing that I am going to visualize and send out in public space... We have learned to be *aware* and think about why that matters. Like, 'Why can't I put *trash* on the street? - Because I have a responsibility'... I really feel that I have some kind of *responsibility* for what I do.

NINA

Do you think that people care?

NOA

Who is 'people'?

NINA
Normal people, non-designers. Does it make a difference for them?

BRITA
They will not see it, but they will *feel* the difference...

NINA
Is it an idealistic view on design?

BRITA
The whole Rietveld education is a *mentality*.

CLAUS
It is very practical. Because that's what we need. I mean, technical stuff, you can always look up somewhere and find out what to do... It is much more important to find out *how* to work with projects.

SIRKEL
The way we study here, is that we *care* about what we do. Whether it is graphic design or not... Like if we would make a café, we would make the best café ever! You know?

NOA
What?

BRITA
If we would? Yeah!

SIRKEL
It is not a nine to five profession...

NOA
Ah! Yeah yeah.

CLAUS
We have to sort of *define* our own personal and professional integrity, - and we don't want to compromise too much.

SIRKEL + NOA
Yeah yeah!

SIRKEL
Let's say that there are two ways of starting a café, I never made one, but I imagine...

NOA
(interrupts)
From the coffee-beans to the furniture...?

SIRKEL (CONT'D)
You can make a café as a business: You figure out what people want, what is trendy at this particular time, you hire the most expensive interior architect and of course you will be successful. But there is also a different way of making a café ... Let's say, if you are really interested in *what* you sell and *how* you make it... Maybe that is the difference?

BRITA
Yes, it comes from another starting point, it is about what is interesting and how to communicate it.

CLAUS
It is about the *intention*

behind it. The choices of a graphic designer will be different than that of someone in advertising... The intention behind is a complex big ... thing. It is more than just ... eh ... that it has to be interesting for *me*, personally as a graphic designer. It has to be interesting *new ways* of doing things... I mean, it is more like a personal attitude to where our *culture* should go ... and ... political aspects ... you know, it is much more personal than advertising.

SIRKEL

Yeah.

CLAUS (CONT'D)

Advertising is almost by definition impersonal, it is not supposed to have the imprint of the *person* who did it. Eh ... it is supposed to communicate to some *non-existing* average consumer...

NOA

(interrupts)

And then ... you know...

CLAUS (CONT'D)

As a graphic designer it is much more about *you*, what you want to put into it... Things that are on your mind or...

SIRKEL

(frowns)

I still think that it is a very *practical* profession, in the sense that the *message* comes

first. That you really convey
the *message*, but you do it
in a special way. A way that
is right for that particular
project!

NOA

Yes, I would like to convey the
message, but in a *transparent*
way ... I mean ... let's say in
an *honest* way, okay?

NOA looks at the others one by one, to make sure
they understand.

NOA (CONT'D)

I am not trying to ... wrap it
and make it into in something
else than what it is.
Marketing is always trying
to *make* things emotional...

BRITA

But they are never ever going
to get there, because it never
starts from the *inside*.

NOA

(almost singing)

If you buy the cheese you will
fall in loooove! Ha ha ha...
Cheese anyone?!

SIRKEL

(laughing)

Ah, yeah, different strategy.

BRITA

(serious)

I think the most successful
way of doing *graphic design*,
in this personal way ... is that
you are *not visible*, you are
visible *through* the fact that

you can make another person look at something in a certain way.

NOA

Yeah...

BRITA (CONT'D)

(exited)

Like Linda's book... Great example... 'Why Mister, Why?'[7] Where this photographer comes and just wants a book with 40 beautiful photos. But they, the designers, where able to make up a whole concept ... and to make his photos communicate in the strongest way they ever could! They chose a much larger collection and also incorporated news-stories so the photos got a context. It was great! ... That the graphic designer can be an *editor*, is really a strength!

CLAUS

That is graphic design in our definition! Some people have the idea that a graphic designer just gets some text and some images and then *lays* it out. But that is just Desktop Publishing. But graphic design *is* also being and *editor* and coming up with the full concept of *how* to solve something, not just ... blindly doing what the client asks.

NOA

That was what we were saying, that Linda and Armand ... That they were able to see what would be good for the photographer,

for the *book*... Here it was better to show *reality* than beauty...

BRITA

That's what I mean! It's just such a clear example, of where it really *works*, where you actually get your voice out so screaming loud of what you are able to do as a graphic designer.

NINA

But in an invisible way?

BRITA

Yeah... just how it should work.

SIRKEL

Here I also think about the article 'Research and Destroy'[8] by Daniel van der Velden[9]... Where he talks about that *real* design is *inventing*! It is not about making a car that *looks* more beautiful, but about *inventing* a car. That is real design! The visuals become shal-low if it they are not related to the *function*.

BRITA

Yeah, like...

SIRKEL

Like... for a book you *invent* how this book could be better - Like with 'Why Mister, Why?'

NINA

When you talk about it, it sounds great, but then *why* is this approach not more apparent in design today?

BRITA

Because other people have different starting points. They don’t *learn* how you do that, they don’t learn how to *see* that. I think we really have to be more designers who thinks in this way, Otherwise we will disappear... Am I too negative in this group?

The others laugh and move around.

NOA

Maybe?

BRITA

But we’re dying, Noa!

Others laughing.

NINA

But why are we dying if this is a good way of designing?

BRITA

It gets eaten up by money... I think it is more interesting how we are going to take graphic design *back* again, you know...

SIRKEL

But hey, come on if you do a book, and you - the designer - want to re-define the whole approach, it takes *time* it takes money, you know all these small things, and ... the world is just so *fast* that there is usually no time for this.

BRITA

It is about *daring* also...

SIRKEL
Of course!

BRITA
Clients don't dare to...

SIRKEL
It comes down to really practical things, not that people don't *want* it, but they don't have time and money and ...

BRITA
(takes over)
They also don't know what to ask, when they don't know what the *possibilities* are...
I mean, the understanding for what we are doing doesn't even exist outside of this department...

NOA
Yeah, yeah, exactly!... You read my mind ... That is what I really wanted to say...

BRITA
I mean, I was once asked to do a poster, and they said they wanted it in *two* days!! In two days they wanted the posters...
And eh ... ah ... hooow?

NOA
Yeah, like I was asked to design a publication, where the client came with all the material. So we took it and we looked at it. And we realized that if there was no possibility to reshoot the photos or ... something, then it was not possible for us to work with it. And we explained it to

... the client and she was like,
(acting when she speaks)
'No no no, I don't have any budget, I already hired a photographer, so the images are done, the text and captions are written and now *your work* is to lay it out.' And then we were like; 'Okay, but then we cannot do it!' And then she was like;'But this is your job isn't it?? You are the designers, right??'

Laughter, comments of disbelief.

SIRKEL

Yeah yeah...

BRITA

Yeah, you are very right, but the *problem* is that people don't know... I, for instance, don't know about photography, I don't know how to take a *good picture*... I can just *see*, I can see a picture and then I can say, okay, that is interesting. But then if I see another picture next to it, then I can maybe see that the *second* photo is better, but if I just see the first one, then I would take that. I would maybe have a weird feeling about it, but I cannot ... judge it...

Pause, thinking.

BRITA (CONT'D)

We - as graphic designers - can whine until we *die*, but we have to make a *difference*, if we want to *exist*.

SIRKEL

But...

NOA

The client we worked with was, really confused because, (laughing a bit while talking) someone had adviced her; ‘Hey! You should document the project, and after that it will be easier ... for the graphic designer to make a publication.’

BRITA

(misunderstands)

But that is a good idea!

NOA

(sighs)

Wait a sec.! Wait a second... Anyway, the problem was that she did not realize that hiring a photographer is making a *design decision*. So when she brought it to us, it was difficult to have any influence... So it could make some kind of sense...

BRITA

But how can we change this? Because this is ... (loud) not - her - own - fault!!!

NOA

We ... we talked to her, and she was really nice, and we explained her why it was difficult to work with.

BRITA

So she actually turned *you* down in the end, then? Because you wanted to re-do the whole thing?

NOA

We said; ‘We feel that for *now*, we cannot help you, you need to find someone else’... Then she said; ‘Hey, this is your job! And most of the time you *are* gonna get the images done already and you are going to get the text done already, so what do you *think* you are going to do as graphic designers?!!’

CLAUS +
SIRKEL

Haha haha...

BRITA

That I *hate*!! When people tell *you* what graphic design is ... FUCK YOU ... really!!!

CLAUS

Aaaah!

BRITA

That I think is *arrogant* ... and ... and really *stupid*! I would never tell an artist, (mocking) ‘You’re supposed to make a painting of me in this and this style!’

The others laugh and agree.

BRITA

It is really annoying when people do that!

NOA

Yeah...

CUT TO

4 INT. RIETVELD - GRAPHIC DESIGN STUDIO - ROOM 217 4

They are sitting at the same table, but have changed seats. The coffee cups and the books on the table are the same, but in different positions. CLAUS has split a small stick (stick used to stear in the coffee) into little pieces and is now putting them in a cup, one by one.

SIRKEL
(gesticulates)
There are so many different things that a designer can do...

NOA
Ah!

BRITA
But we should be involved from the *beginning*! That is always the problem, that they come to us too late!

SIRKEL
Of course!

BRITA
That is what we have to do!

NOA
(talks over BRITA in pure excitement)
Exactly! Exactly exactly exactly!!! COMMUNICATE!!
(claps her hands and stands up)
Exactly! ...

NOA walks back and forth restlessly while talking.

NOA (CONT'D)
The client I worked with should have called a designer to work with her from the beginning, because the problem was that she

did not know what she wanted!
... So there was a room for a
graphic designer to step in
(stepping loudly with her foot)
and to *help* her realize what
kind of material she was dealing
with.

BRITA

Yeah.

SIRKEL

(nodding)

Mmm...

NOA

I think it was a small expe-
rience for her, to actually
realize, what graphic design
deals with, you know...

NOA is standing with her back against the wall.
They talk simultaneously for a few moments.

BRITA

But how can you *prevent* it?
I think *that* is more
interesting...

NOA

Next time, next time!

BRITA

Otherwise this is going to go on
forever!

NOA

(shouting,
gesticulating)

Listen! Listen!

BRITA
We have to think of *how* we can change this!

NOA
Listen! Listen!

BRITA
For the *future*!

NOA
For example this client will know *next* time... Next project...

BRITA
But that is *one* person, we should... Should we just sit and wait for people to come to us???

NOA
What?

BRITA
But we cannot sit around...

NOA
(interrupts)
Hey, what do you want me to say!

BRITA
Hey! Can I finish??

NOA
(defensive)
Yeah...?

BRITA
We cannot sit and *wait* for people to come to us and then we *teach* them?

NOA
(shouting, gesticulates)
But I didn't say that!!!

BRITA
No ... I ...

NOA
(still very loud)
I didn't say it!!!

BRITA
(smiling)
Well, yeah... Okay ... whatever...

NOA
WHAAAT??

BRITA
What I mean, is that this is what is happening to us *all* the time if we don't communicate what our profession deals with *before* they come to us! The problem *now* is that we depend on one person telling another person, who *maybe* tells a third person ...

NOA
(defensive)
Yeah yeah yeah ... I understand!

BRITA
We have to make it *together* ... go out ... in some way ... I don't know that way, but...

NOA
(interrupts)
Okay! But you are asking me, how I can make a change here?

BRITA

No no no, you are giving an example ... and that is just ... an example, look, I am not criticizing what you are saying!

NOA

(sceptic)

Hmm.

BRITA

I am just saying how I see it is working now...

NOA

Yeah yeah...

BRITA

So how could we ... (makes a noise where she sucks in air) mbrrrrsssccccchh!

NOA

(calms down again)

Maybe it is like Claus said, that architects are talking and expressing their opinions, so maybe graphic designers should do that as well?... I don't know - make conventions ... talks, presentations, events, things, you know, to do *something*!

BRITA

(relieved)

Yeah!

CLAUS

And also, so that the public will get more *respect* for what we are doing.

NOA
Yeah, really...

CLAUS
Because that's what happened
to the architects. It really
helped them, I think ...
I think it could really help
graphic designers as well.

General murmur of agreement.

SIRKEL
(frowns)
Maybe I am wrong now, but it
seems to me that architecture
is a *primary* field...

NOA
Yeah, yeah, it is different.

General murmur of disagreement.

SIRKEL
(calm)
Wait wait... In the sense that,
to survive in the wild, you must
have a roof over your head.

NOA
Yeah, it is something different.

SIRKEL (CONT'D)
To ... ehh...

BRITA
Nooo...

SIRKEL
Come on!

NOA
(on SIRKEL's side)
It is different, for sure!

BRITA

But I am also supposed to *create* things...

SIRKEL

But graphic design is sort of *secondary*, in the sense that it is something *extra*. Once we were talking with Unger[10], eh ... in class, when there was this flood ... in ... eh ... argh!??

NOA

Yeah yeah, I know, - in New Orleans.

SIRKEL

Yeah! In New Orleans. People were spreading *messages* there, like; where you can get shelter, work, food, etc. And they were never *designed* which was not *necessary*, because ... everybody could read them anyway! But of course if someone would have designed them, people would have read them *faster*...

NOA

Yeah.

SIRKEL (CONT'D)

So, still design is kind of the secondary...

BRITA

(interrupts)

Yeah, it is not like people *die* from graphic design made *wrong*...

CLAUS

It is about communicating in a *better* way.

BRITA
Yeah, that's true.

CLAUS
So it is still *just* graphic design ...

BRITA
(big gesture)
It is just clothes!

CLAUS (CONT'D)
Something that people can look at or throw away... Architecture is a thing that can really change your behavior.

BRITA
(agitated)
But hey!! Nobody wants to live ... Nobody wants to live in a place where they can just *eat* and *sleep*!!! That's why we have an important function!

SIRKEL
There's *so much* design now, everything is design, and graphic design is just a small part of this ...

BRITA
It is very important!

SIRKEL
But I think it is always about the *content*, you know, because the design is *secondary*, it is always more *what* you say, not about how it *looks*

BRITA
But it is also about *HOW* you say it!

SIRKEL
True ... but ...

BRITA (CONT'D)
(pointing, smiling at SIRKEL)
Yeah, *that* is also content!

SIRKEL
Content!

BRITA
Exactly!

SIRKEL
Come on, I think that there is always a lot of life-saving graphic design, you know like ... eh ...

BRITA
Yeah, yeah, you can choose different angles in graphic design.

SIRKEL
Info-graphics for instance...

BRITA
(interrupts)
Political design...

SIRKEL (CONT'D)
It is about the *content* ... like if your content is the traffic, you must do traffic signs and then it is crucial, then it is a big thing.

NOA
Yeah, wow...

BRITA
Yeah...

SIRKEL
It is about the *content*.

NINA
It is all about the *content*!

NOA
This is the title for today!

SIRKEL
Content.

NINA
Content.

SIRKEL
Aaand content!

They are looking at each other, nodding in agreement.

CUT TO

5 INT. RIETVELD - GRAPHIC DESIGN STUDIO - ROOM 217 5

They are sitting at the same table. The coffee cups and the books on the table are the same, but in a different position.

NINA
Claus, you were talking about architects before, would it be easier for us to work if we, lets say had a higher status?

CLAUS
Yes, that would be much easier!

NOA
(laughing)
Hey, I did not understand the question???

NINA

To... We all sort of agree that it is difficult to get to do the kind of design that we want to do, right?

NOA

Okay.

NINA

Because it is too slow, it is too complicated, these things...

NOA

Yeah.

NINA

So I am asking now; would it be a good thing, if we had a higher status, like some architects, Rem Koolhaas[11] and so on ...

BRITA

Can the question be if people had a higher *knowledge*? ... If people had a higher knowledge about what we are doing, then... Because *status* is more, that we would have star-glow and ... I feel that is not what is interesting...

CLAUS

It is not the goal, but it would help.

BRITA

If people knew, what we do, then we would *automatically* get a status... Of course if you ask me if it would help if we had a higher status, I would say yes, but that is not the *optimal* thing. The important

thing is that people *un-der-stand* what we can do!

NINA

What we can do, how we do it, and what it *takes* to do it...

SIRKEL

I always compare it to one of these old professions, like ... building a house for instance, which is really a special *niche* profession. If somebody builds you a roof for instance, I wouldn't teach them how to build a roof, because I don't know anything about it...

NOA

That's true...

SIRKEL

And I *trust* them and their profession.

NOA

That's true.

SIRKEL

I think if people understand more what we do, then they would have more *trust*...

CLAUS

Yeah, because ... or... It is difficult, because, imagine we were building this *roof* ... You wouldn't want the man you hire to put a roof on your house, to suggest that you should, you know, (laughing) make a funny new *appendix* to the building, on the place where the roof is ... Because

that is sort of some of the things we also do as graphic designers...

BRITA

But I think it is difficult to talk about status in here ... then it becomes like, 'I want Sagmeister[12] to do this because he is Sagmeister!' Status comes *after* the knowledge...

NOA

That is true, but ...

Everybody speaking in loud voices, only CLAUS is audible.

CLAUS

(loud)

But, but we *have* the knowledge!

Everybody shouting at the same time.

NOA

(loud, is almost crawling on to the table in exitement)

We have to realize that graphic design is not a *craft* anymore, it is not *perceived* as a craft!

CLAUS

Yeah!

NOA (CONT'D)

Everybody has a computer, everybody has software, so everybody *thinks* they can make graphic design, you know!

BRITA)

But it is still about that people don't know, - *cannot*

know, what *we* can do with those tools...

CLAUS

Exactly, that is because not a lot of designers are *talking*!

BRITA

Exactly!

CLAUS

And that is just what we have to do!

CLAUS

If we would have more graphic designers who *spoke*, then ... eh ... we could avoid a lot of conflicts with clients who have crazy ideas about graphic design.

BRITA

But still it is about *knowledge*, it is not about status. You don't start with the status, because then it is hollow, it is not the goal!

NINA

So it is not a goal it is a means ...

BRITA

It can be a private goal, eh ... Status is just a difficult word

NOA

(loud)

Semantics, semantics!

CLAUS

(calm)

Of course it is just a word, the important thing is that we get

to *explain* what we do, because
nobody is gonna do it for us.

NINA
But is there not a problem...?
I know that we talk about 'as
graphic designers' we want a
lot of things, but is this what
all designers want?

BRITA
It is about the Rietveld and
this *community* of graphic
designers, it is all about the
Rietveld, it is all about what
we learn here...

They look at each other, thinking.

BRITA (CONT'D)
Yeah... Can we *claim* the whole
graphic design field then?
Because we are calling ourselves
graphic designers...

SIRKEL
(sceptic)
Hey come on...

NOA
Well, if you need a *table* and
you ask three different people:
one will make it for you very
quickly, the other one will make
it very niiiiice and expensive
... you know, the third...

CLAUS
(interrupts)
Yeah! Just like graphic design;
You can have it either *cheap*,
fast or *good* - pick any two!

NOA

What? What?

CLAUS

Yeah, if it is *cheap* and *good*, then it cannot be *fast*, and...

NOA

(interrupts)

Ah, ah! And if you pick *fast* and *cheap* then it is *not* good!

CLAUS

Exactly -and if it is *good* and *fast* then for sure it is *not* cheap...

SIRKEL

Brilliant! So simple...

NOA

It's exactly like that!

CUT TO

6 INT. RIETVELD - GRAPHIC DESIGN STUDIO - ROOM 217 6

They are still immersed in discussion around the table.

SIRKEL

It is about the *love* of the profession, you know. It doesn't matter what you do if you do it with *love*

NOA

Exactly exactly ...

BRITA

People don't know what graphic design is anymore!

SIRKEL

Yeah, in the last years, there has been a lot of talk about the name of the profession ... Also in the article ‘Research and Destroy’ there was talk about whether we should refrase the name of our profession...

BRITA

Maybe if we would change the name of the profession, then people would realize what we can do?... I don’t know... Or we fight it and take the name back!... And eh, *launder* it so that people would know what graphic design is again... We can always refer to so many graphic designers that *don’t* want the same thing that we do ... ‘Aaah, too intellectual, aah, too much bah bah bah.’ You know, *within* our own field!

General agreement and comments.

SIRKEL

Maybe we *do* have to come up with a new name ...

NOA

(gesticulating)

Fuck names!

BRITA

I don’t know if it is the right way, to claim back graphic design – which I would *love* to do.

NOA

That is the subject, of the day, *definitions*!

BRITA (CONT'D)

I am a graphic designer because I still *fight* to keep my name as a graphic designer, in what I do....
But it is really funny, I did not know what graphic design meant when I came to Rietveld!! I got the clue when I was at the interview and then I was like, 'Fuck, this is what I want to do, but I would never call it graphic design'... That's exactly what I thought back then!

SIRKEL

But what would you call it then?

BRITA

I would call it, eh, with the terms I knew back then, eh ... a mix of eh, creative director, designer and artist! I mean, from what I came from. For me now, *this* is graphic design.

NOA

Mmm ...

CLAUS

(as if he has an ace up his sleeve)

I know what to call it!

NOA

What?

CLAUS
(smirking)
Intellectual desktop-publishing!

Next few lines spoken at the same time.

BRITA
(sarcastic)
Yeah, very good CLAUS...

NOA
Yeah? Intellectual WHAT?

BRITA
Creative ... eh...

NOA
What?

CLAUS
Intellectual desktop-publishing!

BRITA
Creative initiative ... yada yada yada!

NOA
Well, that's not really a name is it?

CLAUS
No... Not really.

NOA
(restless)
Hey! Is anybody up for a cigarette break? Just five minutes...?

Others agree, relieved. A lot of hustle and bustle as they leave the room. They continue talking when they walk down the staircase.

CUT TO

7 INT. RIETVELD - GRAPHIC DESIGN STUDIO - ROOM 217 7

They are just settled again, SIRKEL puts his laptop in his bag. Some reach for coffee and cookies.

NINA
So, where does our responsibility go? I mean, of course it's for the visuals, but we are also playing with the idea of being responsible for the *content*.

SIRKEL
But there is no division between them...

NOA
Division between what?

SIRKEL
Between the visuals and the content.

NINA
Do you think other graphic designers see it like that?

SIRKEL
The way we work *here* is not necessarily the way designers work elsewhere.

NOA
Yeah, like with the different carpenters.

SIRKEL
I think it is a question of *honesty* ... of really being *honest* about what you do ...
...

NOA

I'm saying *manifest yourself*! It is much better if each one of us will manifest himself, and maybe also if there is a *group* - here for example or a school that agrees on, let's say, the same *manifestation*? Manifest! It has much more power...

CLAUS

No ... because we are all so dog-...

BRITA

(takes over, loud)

DogMA! Dogmatist! DogMA!

NOA

(gesticulates)

DOGMA!!

SIRKEL

No, we *cannot* manifest graphic design for the rest of the world, because we're only *students* and we don't know so much...

NINA

(leans back)

Then there are people like Stuart Bailey[13], who seems to have a very reflected perception of the profession, but he has also been practicing graphic design for many years... We are just young and ... *naive*...

CLAUS

(frowns)

But maybe that *is* a good position to have, when you are

writing a manifest about graphic design?...

SIRKEL
Of course, it *has* to be like that ... you should be young and angry and...

BRITA
(smiling)
We are!!!

SIRKEL (CONT'D)
You know Kristjan[14] - who studied here at Rietveld and went back to Estonia - the first thing he did was that he wrote a really long article[15], 16 pages for an Estonian art magazine. He basically wrote that graphic design in Estonia is shit...

NOA
(interrupts)
And everybody read it?

SIRKEL
Yeah, that is *why* he's teaching now!

Laughter, approving comments.

SIRKEL (CONT'D)
Everything changed because of that article... But if he talks about it *now* he is also saying that, yeah ... he has...

NOA
He has a different way of talking about it, right?

SIRKEL
Yeah, he's older and he has more experience...

NOA
(takes over)
Yeah, we should not be afraid of using our *naivety* and ask stupid questions.

BRITA
Yes, we have to do it *now*, when should we do it otherwise?

CLAUS
But Stuart is also not pretending to have all the answers...

NOA
But that's a *different* naivety. That is a naivety that comes from *experience*.

CLAUS
It is interesting with this *naivety* of the graphic designer, because you need to know both this ... *cynical* idea of how the system works and you also need to stay *naive*, because that is the only way to stay *fresh* and *responsive* to each situation... In advertising there were - in my experience - so many systems and templates that you *used* to do something. You took the best way of doing something and then you applied it to *everything*. So everything looked the *same* because it was all done by the best system, - by the fastest, cheapest, best outcome-system.

That was really a bad thing, because things got to look so much *alike* and be so ... so *identity-less*. You have to be aware of not getting habits. Habits in graphic design is a very bad thing ... (laughing) Unless it's good habits, like getting up in the morning and start working.

NOA

So? Why are you saying this?

CLAUS

I'm just saying that some things become bad habits because they don't *provoke* you into *thinking* about what you are actually doing, and it's a very ... very dangerous thing to do.

NOA

But if you are referring to someone who is using, let's say just Helvetica, then ...

Laughter, everybody knows what NOA is hinting at.

BRITA

No, no no! There is a big difference in how Experimental Jetset use it. Because they are consequent and have an idea behind it, that's why it's working!

NOA

(loud)

That's what I wanted to say! If you allow me to finish the sentence.

BRITA
Okay-okay-okay...

CLAUS
I think it's just about being *conscious* about what you do.

Others agree and nod.

CLAUS
And you have to be aware of that a client often will try to impose a *system* on you and will want you to work in a specific way.

SIRKEL
Of course, but for the client there is also a lot of practical things because he is *investing* in you. So there is a lot of *trust* involved. Sometimes all they want is a *service*. They don't want a *friend* to have a beer with, in a pub, you know.

BRITA
I see where you're heading!

SIRKEL (CONT'D)
In the sense that, *we* are more working in the way that we will get *together* with a client and talk about...

BRITA
(interrupts)
Yeah, but you can do the talking in a strictly professional way also - without the beer.

NINA
Do you need to be friends with the client to work for them?

Everybody talking in loud voices at the same time.

CLAUS
I think you are talking about the *intimacy* and the closeness. You don't have to be actual friends with them.

SIRKEL
It's a metaphor ... for that you have to be close to really *understand* the content.

NINA
And you keep *talking* until you understand?

SIRKEL
Yeah! For instance in an advertising agency the designer never *meets* the client!

NOA
What?

SIRKEL
The *designer* never meets the *client*! The art director and the sales manager meets the client ...

BRITA
That is the problem!

CUT TO

8 INT. RIETVELD - GRAPHIC DESIGN STUDIO - ROOM 217 8

They are immersed in discussion, NOA is balancing on her chair, looking at the ceiling.

NINA
I guess we need to be more active in ... showing and

talking about design, maybe we need some more ... *academic* people talking about graphic design?

NOA straightens up and everybody starts yelling No, no no!

NINA
(laughing)
Not in...

SIRKEL
(interrupts)
The point is doing *practical* projects, that you can show to people afterwards.
I don't want to use the word promote, but let's say to *educate* people about graphic design has to be by *making* graphic design, you can't be talking about it in an academic way...

General agreement.

CLAUS
(convinced)
I think graphic designers can and *should* talk about it, as graphic designers who talk about graphic design!

Again everybody talking at the same time.

BRITA
Yeah, you have to show *and* talk about it ... but before you get the problems!

CLAUS
But that is no problem! I mean we are already *making* the

graphic design, we just have to start *talking* about it!

BRITA

Exactly!

NOA

Huh?

NINA

What were you saying?

CLAUS

We are already doing the graphic design, we just have to start talking about it also.

BRITA

This is talking about it, what we are doing right now!

SIRKEL

Yeah, I guess we just need to keep doing that.

NOA

Yeah.

CLAUS

Definetly.

FADE TO BLACK

THE END

NOTES TO THE TEXT

1.
THE GERRIT RIETVELD ACADEMY
Amsterdam, The Netherlands.
www.gerritrietveldacademie.nl

2.
LINDA VAN DEURSEN
Dutch graphic designer, works together with Armand Mevis in design-duo Mevis & van Deursen since 1987. Head of the graphic design department at the Gerrit Rietveld Academy.

3.
THE BASIC YEAR
General foundation year at the Gerrit Rietveld Academy.

4.
EXPERIMENTAL JETSET
Dutch graphic design trio, founded in 1997. Danny van den Dungen and Marieke Stolk teach at the Gerrit Rietveld Academy.

5.
JULIA BORN
Swiss graphic designer, based in Amsterdam. Teaches at the Gerrit Rietveld Academie.

6.
RENÉ PUT
Dutch graphic designer. Teaches at the Gerrit Rietveld Academie.

7.
WHY MISTER WHY? IRAQ 2003–2004
by Geert van Kesteren, designed by Mevis & van Deursen, 2005. Published by Artimo. ISBN 90-8546-016-6.

8.
RESEARCH AND DESTROY
Article by Daniël van der Velden in Metropolis M, no. 2, 2006. See also www.metahaven.net

9.
DANIEL VAN DER VELDEN
Dutch graphic designer and text-writer, works with Maureen Mooren. Advising researcher at the Jan van Eyck Academie in Maastricht, The Netherlands.

10.
GERARD UNGER
Dutch type designer. Teaches at the University of Reading, UK, is Professor of Typography at the University of Leiden. Taught at the Gerrit Rietveld Academy until 2007.

11.
REM KOOLHAAS
Dutch architect, theorist and urbanist. Principal of OMA, and AMO, co-founded 'Volume Magazine'.

12.
STEFAN SAGMEISTER
Austrian graphic designer, based in New York.

13.
KRISTJAN MÄNDMAA
Estonian graphic designer. Teaches graphic design at the Estonian Academy of Arts. Studied at the Gerrit Rietveld Academy 2001–2002.

14.
SHIT OR INTERESTING THINGS IN ESTONIAN GRAPHIC DESIGN
Article by Kristjan Mändmaa in Kunst.ee, no. 3, 2002.

15.
STUART BAILEY
British graphic designer and writer. Edits and designs Dot Dot Dot. Has taught at the Gerrit Rietveld Academie.

FOR FURTHER READING AND DEBATES ABOUT GRAPHIC DESIGN

DESIGN OBSERVER
Online blog. Writings on design and culture.
www.designobserver.com

FIRST THINGS FIRST 2000
A design manifesto.
www.xs4all.nl/~maxb/ftf2000.htm

LIMITED LANGUAGE
Web site dedicated to exploration of design.
www.limitedlanguage.org

RESEARCH AND DESTROY
by Daniël van der Velden in Metropolis M, no.2, 2006.
www.metahaven.net

SPEAK UP
Online forum dedicated to discuss graphic design.
www.underconsideration.com/speakup

STATEMENT OR I'M FRIGHTENED
by Roger Bridgman in Dot Dot Dot no. 3.
www.dot-dot-dot.nl

WHAT IS A DESIGNER
by Norman Potter. Published by Hyphen press, 2002, ISBN 0-907259-16-2.

COLOPHON

CONCEPT AND GRAPHIC DESIGN
Nina Støttrup Larsen

TRANSCRIPTION
Anna Katsina Friis
Katrin Maria Klingner
Nina Støttrup Larsen

PRINTING
Veenman Drukkers

SPECIAL THANKS
Linda van Deursen

THANKS TO
Danny van den Dungen
Anna Katsina Friis
Will Holder
Katrin Maria Klingner
Brita Lindvall
René Put
Noa Segal
Indrek Sirkel
Claus Eggers Sørensen

PUBLISHER
Veenman Publishers/Gijs Stork
Sevillaweg 140
3047 AL Rotterdam- NL
t. +31 10 245 3333
f. +31 10 245 3344
info@veenmanpublishers.com
www.veenmanpublishers.com

ISBN 90-8690-100-5

DISTRIBUTION

D.A.P.
155, Sixth Avenue, 2nd floor
New York, NY 10013, USA
t. +1 212 627 1999
dap@dapinc.com

Idea Books
Nieuwe Herengracht 11
1011 RK Amsterdam-NL
t. +31 20 622 6154
idea@ideabooks.nl

Art Data12,
Bell Industrial Estate
50 Cunnington Street
W4 5HB London- UK
t. +44 20 8747 1061
info@artdata.co.uk

Nowadays, if we speak about graphic design we can never be sure if we are actually talking about the same thing. The books in this series investigate different fields of graphic design where this lack of definition currently exists, as a means to contribute to the discussion and awareness of an arbitrary profession.

HARD SCHOOL BOOKS
Graphic design department,
Gerrit Rietveld Academie,
Amsterdam, June 2007